LO DEATH AND BAD BEHAVIOUR

A CELEBRATION IN VERSE

J.X. COUDRILLE

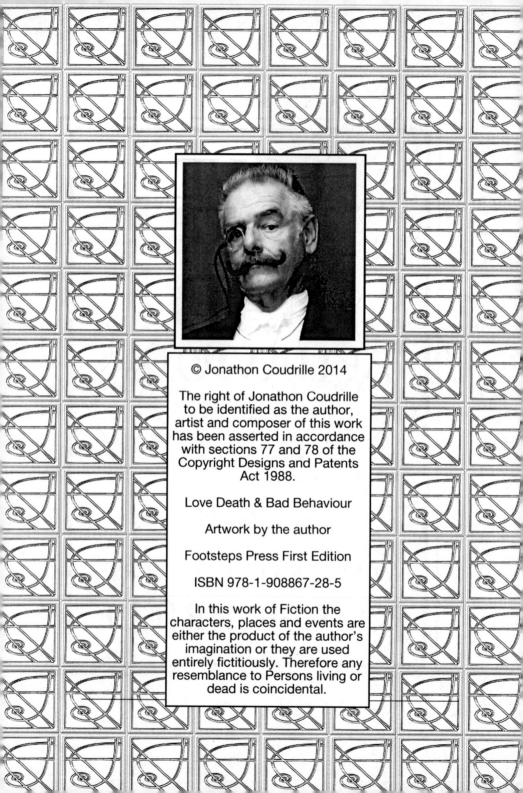

Love Death & Bad Behaviour

Artwork by the author

Footsteps Press First Edition

ISBN 978-1-908867-28-5

LOVE DEATH
AND,
BAD BEHAVIOUR

A CELEBRATION IN VERSE
J. X. COUDRILLE

CONTENTS

LOVE, DEATH
AND
BAD BEHAVIOUR

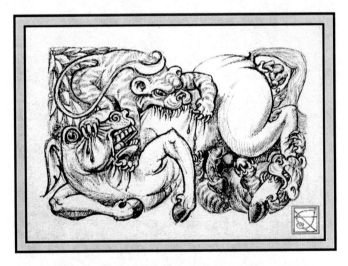

DEDICATED TO HUMAN-KIND AND,
THAT IMPOTENT OLD ASS DEMOCRACY

FOR FELIX DENNIS (1947-2014)

PREFACE

LOVE, DEATH AND, BAD BEHAVIOUR.
PREFACE TO THE 2014 EDITION.

Song invaded my mind very early. As I dozed in my father's Punch and Judy booth in our painted caravan, the voices of my parents soared over the rumble of the wheels and underscored my dreams as does today's ever-on television underscore those of the cossetted generation. My mother sang along with - and, as a throaty alternative to - the sibilant clangour from a leatherette-bound portable wind-up gramophone that was our sole source of recorded music in my pre-school years on the road; at some point the gramophone was augmented by a 'portable' radio not much smaller than a car-battery (powered by a battery not much smaller than a car) that granted us whistling access to the BBC Home Service and, the Light Programme. Also, depending on our location, to the slightly racier programmes from Radio Luxembourg, an early commercial radio station on the American pattern that was financed by its sponsors whose advertisements provided what was at that time, novel punctuation.

Small children in that ration-book bordered world went to bed while the June sun blazed unfairly down beyond the curtains, but I was allowed to listen to the primitive boy-soap "Dan Dare, Space Pilot" if I gagged down the sudsy malted milk drink that paid for my pleasure. I can smell it now.

I remember – I suspect my father helped me; he had already made my first guitar out of orange-box wood and very stinky boiled glue - building a simple Crystal set that, with Government-Surplus headphones secreted under my pillow, meant I could listen without drinking the drink, and sneak in to the rest of the airtime – No, radio was not 24 hours then – which was filled with instrumental polkas, rumbas, quicksteps and foxtrots and, songs with melting vocals by Dick Haymes and less meltingly, Joseph Locke. Vera Lynn majestically contemplated the White Cliffs of Dover. American Idols sang greater songs with hotter bands and, lesser stars were horribly lumbered by their unfeeling producers with depressing novelty numbers like "MairzydoatsandDozydoatsandliddleLamzeydivey" the idiocy of which would not be surpassed until poor Guy Mitchell had to sing "Feet up, pat him on the Po-po" till that cringe-making masterpiece too was eclipsed by "GillyGillyOssenpfefferKatzenellenBogenbytheSea!" It's a wonder I became an adult, let alone a musician.

But the Gramophone also played finer things. Sometimes the needle scratched around the leader-groove until it found, not the intoxicating "Voodoo Moon" by Carmen Cavallaro or the – to me, disappointing, tho' for a while my father's favourite - "Bloop, bleep" by Danny Kaye, but a fine Shakespearian voice like a baritone woodwind (Gielgud? Olivier?) reading Walter de la Mare:

"Slowly, silently, now the moon, Walks the night in her silver shoon;. This way, and that, she peers, and sees. Silver fruit upon silver trees..."

I was transported, and asked for the record to be played in preference to the romping sound tracks from Dumbo and Pinocchio, the day's Disney Blockbusters that had been bought for my delectation.

My personal affair with Euterpe and Erato waited but a few years and grabbed me while I was still prepubescent. By this time my father was a fledged Ventriloquist, "topping the bill" (as we used to call Headlining) and writing comic lyrics for his television shows and cartoon films. Money was ours, the horse was long retired, the caravan sold – my mother had 'gone off' it when I knocked all my milk-teeth out on the step after my father left us in a field in Wales where it rained solidly for a summer while he went to Egypt - and we now had a cabin on the cliffs, a Gothic house near Stratford and a roaring Ford Vee-Eight. He would urge this up the hills with the action of his hips as he had the horse rather than change gears, which he considered stuff for sissies. On the down-hills he would knock the overheated brute out of gear altogether and coast terrifyingly through the screaming wind shouting improvised parodies and belting out the choruses on his mouth-organ, often keeping time with the hooter. Fortunately there was little traffic in nineteen forty-nine. I, squashed between this ebullient jongleur and my now fashionable and scented mama on the American

Cloth of the seat, also joined in, finding that verse came easily, my treble completing this anarchic take on the von Trapp archetype.

My first written piece was strictly metric, accurately rhymed and, deeply profound. It was called 'Mick the Moochy Pooch', and concerned a pet dog that smoked cigars. It could be sung – as could most of my father's songs - to the melody of 'The Yellow Rose of Texas' and it left the audience dry-eyed, as did my follow-up, 'Jake the Spiv' who carried a Shiv and stuck it in a Teddy-Boy who Didn't Live. This unfortunate had an improbable name that I'd made up to rhyme with Wednesday after my mother pointed out that the market in which the killing had taken place was closed on Monday, my first choice because it rhymed with Grundy.

I persevered, learned notation and, concocted my own melodies, so that by the time I was thrown out of my second Art School I was ready to catch the Satire boom of the 1960s and thrill West Country television viewers with immortal lines like

'Any Beatnik they find with a concave behind will be run out of town by and by...'

As often happens, the demand (believe it!) for what one announcer referred to as my "scurrilous ditties" proved to be Improving, and I moved to London where I regularly appeared, if that is the word within Radio, on the Today programme in the lighter-hearted days of the charming Jack de Manio, before moving back into Television and the delights of Music Proper that didn't depend on a jokesy lyric line. In the half-century since, I've written constantly, and have rifled my pile of mouldering notebooks as well as a succession of cobwebbed word-processors for this collection. I see that I was unable, as a young man, to write love-songs.

I have since learned much. I hope you enjoy the destination as much as I have enjoyed the journey.

Cornwall 2014

LOLLIPOPS

LOLLIPOPS

HOW OFTEN
CATS ARE NOT FOR CUDDLING!
QUEEN'S PARK
BIO 1985
KENNING THE LIZARD
SHOULD MY...
THIS YEAR THE ALPS...

'LOLLIPOPS' was the term the British conductor and card Sir Thomas Beecham used for the lighter items in the repertoire that he 'threw to the audience' as encores.

The suggestion of trivia, lightness and sweetness is worth a little misappropriation, and so I've used it to corral these few items which are: are fairly trivial, fairly sweet... although 'This Year The Alps...' owns a little salt and vinegar.

I've also included my only Kenning poem. Most of my rhymes are contemporary in feel and form, as I've not the scholarship nor leisure to write otherwise, but the Kenning is an old idea, Ninth Century at a guess. I understand that calling one's ship 'Wave's Horse', one's sword 'Skull-Cleaver' or one's penis by any of the many base-word-plus-determinant couplings that still survive in speech today* rated as high wit with the Vikings. And, rightly.

Cornwall 2014

The vintage low-life broadcast Comedy "Hancock's Half-Hour" was rich in urban Kennings (underlined):

1

'You're looking for a <u>bunch of fives</u> round the <u>fag-hole, Mate</u>!' which translates as,
'Friend, continue as you are and I may be constrained to shut your mouth with a fist.'
To disambiguate, in British English street slang, a "fag" was a cigarette. In UK boys'-school slang a fag is a junior that, in return for protection and perquisites waits as a personal servant upon a Senior. This latter is not the definition intended.

HOW OFTEN

How often does one yearn within a kiss
For unexpected, overwhelming bliss?

How likely, in this life of scams and schemes
Reality more wondrous than one's dreams?

How frequently the game of grooms and brides
Results in disappointment. On BOTH sides...

But now, my Love, the fantasy comes true,
And sweeter far... The blissful dream is:
                                          You

Cornwall 2014

3

CATS ARE NOT

CATS ARE NOT FOR CUDDLING.
Unhand me, if you please.
How DARE you misappropriate
The Queen of All She Sees!
My tail is set a-quiver;
Don't I bristle at your touch?

But oh!
You've brought some liver...
Why,
I love you
VERY
much.

Cornwall 2011

KENNING ONE

Soft-dawning
Shrub-spawning
Chamomile-lawning
Spirit stealer;
Depth-plundered
Cave-wondered
Surf-thundered
Soul healer

Snake-mothering
Haste-smothering
Taste-othering
Holy-fable,
Boat-sailing
Hay-baling
Cloud-trailing
Solar-table

Car-flocking
Tractor-blocking
Emmet-mocking
Road-winder;
Lark-dancer
Life enhancer
Echo-answer:
Soul-finder

Bat-flitter
Linnet-twitter
Nest-sitter
Chough-pecker!

Gale-sweeping
Watch-keeping
Widow-weeping
Ship-wrecker.

Croust-sharing
Sea-faring
Ore-bearing
Wizard and gnome

West-setting
Fish-netting
Tea-getting
Done fretting
Time-forgetting
Merlin-flying
Gull-crying
Peregrine-spying
Kestrel and buzzard
The Lizard,
Cornwall,
My home.

Cadgwith 2014

5

QUEEN'S PARK

Queen's Park. Morning. I remember
Very well. It was September
And the ice-cream chimes have just begun.
Certainly the day is very warm...
And round the bend of once-green bushes,
Spruce and natty like the milk float
That is blocking off my sun
Comes Adam Faith, decidedly the boss.
Tightly Suited, strutting strongly
60s haircut lacquered to a fine complacent gloss
Swaggering outrageous padded shoulders,
A flaring fair young woman clinging to his arm.
But, I see I've read it wrongly.
He in fact is also slender
Younger, of a different gender
And the suit is vintage splendour
So it isn't 1967
In the fall
After all
But free and splendid Summer
In Nineteen Eighty-One.

Queen's Park, 1981

SEPTEMBER 1985

How shall I announce to you
My callow immaturity?
By turning up my stereo,
That sounds of gross impurity
Fill up my street
And there, belabour
Even the ears
Of my farthest deafest neighbour.

Then too, my choice of voice,
Yet louder, meaner,
Bursts from the windows
Of my green Cortina!

Thus do I transcend
With absolute security
My adolescent, hardly pleasant,
Unrelieved obscurity

Diss, 1985

7

SHOULD MY

Should my physiognomy stay fuzzy
Like a fox,
Or should I mow my whiskers
With the little buzzing box?
The quandary involves, of course,
My appetite for flattery,
But mainly it revolves
Around the juice left
In the battery...

I
Had a beard of two decades,
A noble growth and,
Tough.
It hid the lines of bitterness
I formed when life was
Rough...
It hid my inner weakness, my capacity for pain
But maybe there are qualities I'd like to see again?

Some humour and some kindness
May have left an imprint there
Consigned to dismal blindness by
That undergrowth of hair...

For better or for worse,
Come! Burst your final amp to shave me
And show the waiting mirror
What I've made of what God gave me.
Postscript:

And yes, the mirror told me I'd committed something rash;
I'd better speak my lines betimes beneath a wide moustache...

Highgate 1979

THIS YEAR

This year the Alps
Can keep their draughty heights.
No precipice, no pass, no peak
Shall call me from the hearth
Where, drowsy lamplight nights
In idle peace
Shall I, redundant sprawl.
With book and glass to hand
For true delight.

This year, content
I'll view the misty stars through British windows.
Traffic jams at Chur
Athletic youth
In horrid German cars
Can carve each other up
On bends obscure.
Their destiny will be no part of ours.

This year, not even sober and aware
The ghastly midnight breakneck
Of the Tschuggen
Shall I, in parody of courage dare,
A lunatic upon a child's toboggan!
No Apres-Ski, no stress no debt,
No lemming-headed dawn roulette
And only very slight... regret;

Beneath a greyer Island sky
And with a kinder inner eye
This year I'll view the mountains
From my chair.

Diss 1988,

PASTORALES

PASTORALE

A PASTORALE is: "A composition evocative of rural life characterized by moderate compound duple or quadruple time and sometimes having a droning accompaniment"

Well, the droning accompaniment is familiar to poets who read in venues where conversation has the better of attention, but my Number One here, 'FLIES' deliberately and firmly demands an insectile backdrop from the audience. The short verse certainly deals with one of the concomitants of living – or eating – in the countryside: uninvited critters at – or on – one's table, and given that there are some hundred and seventy million insects to each human being on our beautiful planet, it's natural that they sneak into a few of these verses as they do into the marmalade. But I must not trivialise the Life Rural. Apart from a Quarter Century based in London while I travelled the world as a professional musician, I've had the wonderful fortune to live in rural Britain for most of my life, mostly Cornwall tho' my first school was at Ilmington in the Cotswolds. The Spider in 'SOLSTICE' is not an insect. Insects have only six legs. With a hundred and seventy million insects each, we should be glad.

CornwalL 2011

13

FLIES

Two Flies, devoid of delicacy, decency or tact
Performed upon my luncheon tray the procreative act.
Quite without contrition, they refused to call a halt,
    Intent upon coition,
      'Though I peppered them with salt.

    At length the She-Fly wearied
      Of his passionate attack
      And shook her paltry partner
      Like a raincoat
      From her back...

    Bemused, distrait, diverted.
   He lay there scarcely spent
To be pulled along inverted
Like a clown
  When off she went.

    Her trampled wings she mastered
      Looking flustered as she fled
      And dropped
      The little bastard
      In the Mustard
      On
      His
     H
      e
       a
        d

St. John's Wood 1985

AN AUGUST REVERIE

Some distant passing sound,
Some scent or taste,
Some accident of dappled light
Is printed
Deep
Within the matrix of the brain.

No sleep-insistent dream is found
Yet I am graced,
Bound with a vision
Sweet and bright,
And motionless as once was any Sunday Afternoon.

The drowsy wind-warped silk
Of waving grain.

The rusty creaking
Of a gate or chair
And Childhood's eye
Will focus on it still:
The sun-stitched patchwork
Of a Cornish hill,
The dusty,
Bell-rich
August Teatime air
Crowned with the sound of windmills,
Drowned in the drone of Evensong,
The creeping dusk and rising harvest moon.

Cadgwith 1980s

I CAN SCARCELY BELIEVE

The heat of the sun
The mildness of the day

I saw an ice-pink rose
In vulnerable bloom
High upon its leafless thorn
Across a crumbling wall

An inch away
From belching city traffic's leaded boom
False Spring
Has pulled the threads
That cause the saffron flowers
And all the pulsing writhing buds
To rise
Above
The Rain-moon
And its old accustomed
Sodden footed
Gloom.

Hampstead 1980s

I WANDERED OUT
ONE AUGUST DAWN

I wandered out one August dawn, and,
Heedless of the clock,
I stayed to watch the sunrise warm a lichen-tufted rock...
So stridently botanical
The fume of earth and rain; that
Reverie required no craft to quiet my tumbling brain.
    Aslant a podded plant that
        Nodded level with my head
            A tiny grub depended from a microscopic thread...

And if I may address You thus,
One who made us all,
to swim and fly, stand, sit and lie,
To run and climb and crawl,
Why did you make some things so BIG
And some so very small?

No bigger than a mustard-seed,
More slender than a pin,
A tiny dot of consciousness, to eat, excrete and spin.
A millimetre acrobat
Conditioning my eye
Prepares me to be startled by a mighty, half-inch fly...

While fathoms from my footprints
In the boundless sucking sea
Rolls vast and dark
A Basking Shark
Ten times the size of me.
So, if I may address You,
Who made rock and wave and cloud,
Who spreads the snow so white below
And makes the thunder loud,
Whose logic even I can see, in root and branch and twig,
Why did you make some things so _{small,}

And some

so very

BIG?

St.Ives 1960s

LENT, THE SLOW FAST

It's Thursday, and the second day of Lent:
The grim grey gale rakes plant and bird and sky;
The weightless gulls blown sideways in alarm
Indignant in their freezing discontent
Treat the rattling windows to their guano,
More permanent, less welcome than their cry.

The morning crow, his flight an awkward hook
Ironic as his croak, that jerks, still loud
In dins of shaken shrub aslant the farm
Must hurtle jagged angles to the brook.
Dots that might be leaves and might be jackdaws
Cavort upon the tossing fallen cloud.

All the Helichrysum stems are broken
Shivering cobwebs on the windward beat
By whipping spray and clots of salted foam.
The ailing stove makes angry burps of smoke
Ruffling stretched and sleeping cats that dream
Dark fantasies of freshly bleeding meat.

Out on the lumped horizon can be seen
Like sticking plasters on the battered sea,
Like memories of love that once was warm:
Small rushed repairs of sunlight, grey and green
Distant as the sugar and the butter

That clutter

The crockery from Tuesday's Pancake Tea.

St. Grada 2011

19

ON RETURNING

This late October morning
Soothes my soul
As only England can
The silent sun
At eyebrow height
Enchants me
From my aching bones
To the distant rim
Of the dewy-turf and wild-herb scented
Breeze-borne bell and Songbird-sounding
Squirrel-scampered
Blue-receding world.

Magpies,
Bright as Eton Scholars,
(long tail-coats
And stiff white collars)
Cross my path repeatedly
In couples, twos and pairs.

Money spiders
In their dozens,
More informally
Than cousins
Climb upon me merrily
For exercise and air.
The earth beneath my feet,
The World beneath my seat
Rumbles grandly
On her slanting axis.
The Half-Moon clocks
The Equinox.
The distant wind-wound bell
Weaves a sudden chill
Among the browning oak-leaves

The year turns the corner
And Autumn
Turns her cheek.

Kenwood House 1981

21

SOLSTICE

I rose to watch the sun this solstice dawn.
With mindless tender interfering care
I saved an ailing, fretting butterfly:
Released it from the cobweb of its fate,
The doom of bonds as strong as damsel hair.
It cleaned itself and fluttered to the sky
A dwindling dot of freedom high above
Far brighter in the blue than any bird;
Its brilliant paean to liberty and love
– As, worshipping, I watched it from the lawn –
Entranced me. And, I never knew or heard
The spider's dark arachnid curse of hate.

Carn Barrow 2006

THREE SKIES

SKY ONE

Bright dappled waters
Bird pierced
Pieced with sunlight
Blue for life, fortuity –
Enamelled winter sky
High and clear

SKY TWO

Ice marbled waters
Frost laced
East of daylight
White for death, for purity
A blanket-shrouded sky
Dim and near

SKY THREE

Deep silent waters
Rain-dark
Greased with streetlight
Black for pain, maturity.
I cannot see the sky.
You're not here.

Moscow 1991

THE CORMORANT

Silent as a snake the Cormorant keeps its eyes
On the waves that thrash and break
From precipice to horizon,
Its attitude more pensive than the owl.

I ventured 'Tell me, black, aquatic fowl,
Your reverie intrigues me. Does the day
Inspire you with its grandeur?'
'Grandeur! Nay!' replied the bird.
'Fish, fish!! My constant thought
Concerns the fish I'll catch and,
Those I've caught and when,
On days like this the sea is rough –
I wonder if I'll ever catch enough.

The sort I favour most are plump, and sound –
About eight inches long and, six around
And, give or take an ounce, they weigh a pound.

On them I dote. They fit my throat, I've found.
And it is right, and fitting
That my mind should dwell on fish,
For the sort that I describe,
(And you may ask them if you wish)
Are not inclined to muse upon the beauties of the sea;
Indeed, they dwell obsessively
On Cormorants
Like
Me.'

Highgate 1980s

24

OF LOVE AND DEATH

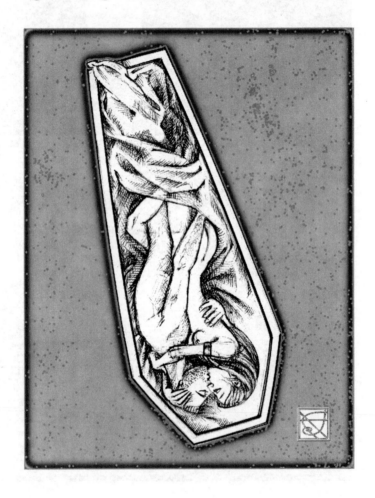

OF LOVE AND DEATH

Birth and Death are the great fixed stars in our Universe.

Love is the Comet that blazes in on the wildest of parabolas to knock our ordered Galaxy apart. Very rarely does it fail to transform, and there's no surprise that it has forever been the burden of Song.

Love can grow from sapling-soft beginnings until it is a mighty tree, or it can slam in with the subtlety of an avalanche, knocking such trees flat; we can be comfortably celibate, blissfully betrothed, (only a generation ago these afflictions went hand in hand) we can even be solidly wedded, when suddenly love of an undreamed and terrifying beauty sweeps in and takes us by force, splattering bliss and heartbreak across whole communities and making scoundrels of the most faithful and dutiful amongst us.

I shamefacedly grab this opportunity to beg forgiveness for the pain and damage I have caused and the hearts I have broken, and to offer it unequivocally to those that have broken mine.

Love is: a very serious business but, few of us would wish never to experience it.

In this respect it differs markedly from Death.

Some of these poems are newly cultivated, some culled from the rag-bag of the last half century; 'Parks his Ferrari' was written in Saint Ives in the 1960s as a bawdy song and (somewhat) redacted. I've included another song in this chapter: 'Mexico' because it was written as a poem and I subsequently set and harmonised it for performance with the band. As is the way of things, 'Mexico' was then recorded as a wordless instrumental.

Cornwall 2014

THE LOST POEM

The sky is moonless dark, the summer old
And quilted casket-close the thought of bed
The room is airless, dry, yet strangely cold...
Uneasily I rise. My steps are led
Past moth-grey tapestry and muffled ticking clock
Past tarnished picture frame and cobwebbed chair
And step by echoing step and tick by tock
My feet uncertain on the creaking stair
Night-flagged shadows on a stone-chilled floor
Paint by peeling plaster, brick by block
Eyeless window crowding mouthless door
Protesting oil-starved hinge and sticking lock;

The pavement's grit abrades the fading night
An empty beer can in the gutter's heat
With mocking halo in the sickly light
Goes rattling down the subway-rumbled street

I coax my lean old sporting car awake
Metal, air and fire, the food of flight...
I check the yawning dials, release the brake,
And growling happily she seeks the Northern Height.

The clouds are purple and the dawn sprays gold
On child-climbed statue, bird-stained bench
And dog-fouled tree
The timid tender sunbeams tease and then enfold
The beaded grass, the iron gates, and me.

I pass in silence down the gravelled way
The tumbled urns reflect the smiling sky
And as the city turns to greet the day,
I kiss the stone, my Darling, where you lie.

Highgate

"...AND, HAVING PUT MY HEART ON SHOW,"

Girl!
What am I to say
Of my crazy love for you?
Only that since I first beheld your grace and, in those hours
Breathed in the light from your strange unworldly eyes,
Basked in the radiance of your wide and perfect smile,
My helpless heart - and, all that it empowers -
Is simply, yours.

My life has ever been a rich and full affair,
But now,
I swear,
Despite the many cares and fascinations,

There is
No part
Of any walking day,
No part of any sleepless night,
No part
Of any waking dream,
That is not filled,
And filled in all dimensions,
With my loving thoughts of you.

Well, yes, the teasing tyranny
Of that old fraud Desire
Has far too often overcome my sense;
But you, my longed-for One
Have simply: set my soul on fire.
And there: I rest the case for the defence.

...And having put my heart on show,
I seek a glimpse of yours:
Is it really far too high,
I Let my fine opinion fly?
Drowned in such love,
(One drowns when one adores...)
Be comforted. Be easy, for:
Though foolish I am NOT a fool;
Perfect? Well, of course you're not; (we all accrue our flaws...)
Yet; wonderful and more you are.
A plangent honesty crowns loveliness with truth,
And truer than the norm by far ,
In truth,
That crown, is
Yours.

Bodmin Moor

MEXICO

I didn't go to Mexico,
Nor saw the sunrise through your hair
Lightly tangled round my fingers
On some strange, none too fresh pillow,
Armadillo in my arms.
I shield you from the dawn;
You yawn
And turning, smile.

Why is it that, of all the ways
That lovers lie, (their loving done
For now at least) this image lingers?
Laurence Harvey, lying dying
Fondly called it Playing Spoons.
I feel your trusting spine
In mine
This yearning while...

> Oh, how I longed for Mexico,
> Wrong that I didn't get to go
> So wrong, but how was I to know?
> I've so much to answer for...
> Never to consecrate the bed,
> Nor say what needed to be said...
> Time now to celebrate the dead
> For a world that is no more.

I ought to go to Mexico;
I journey very far alone,
With lovers, too, that brought – and bring
Their very different minds and faces;
Places that I scarce recall.
We said we'll keep in touch.
As such,

We don't too much, I find...
And can I go to Mexico?
The pictures that I treasure glow
Where you are Frida Kahlo, singing
And I gallop like a hero,
My sombrero understood,
A Six-Gun Robin Hood
That Hollywood
Designed

        Oh, how I longed for Mexico,
        Wrong that I didn't get to go
        So wrong, but how was I to know?
        I've so much to answer for...
        Never to consecrate the bed,
        Nor say what needed to be said...
        Time now to celebrate the dead
        For a world that is no more.

I must not go to Mexico
For it was over long ago
The mission bells ought to be ringing
While you kiss your Caballero.
Broken-hearted, I'm resigned
(relieved, perhaps?)
To find
My Mexico,
Is of the mind.

Lausanne 1993

MY MOTHER LOVED MY FATHER

My mother loved my father
In a valley by the sea
Where primrose and forget-me-not
And tangled wildwood grew...
The cottage rough; the food? Enough
Though not enough for three.
She dreamed her child
Amid the dew
When I was yet to be.

My father loved my mother
On a hill among the stones
Where curved Horizons blurring sea and cloud spread out
To view
Cold sunlight where the lizards lie
And glitter at the windy sky
Heat is in the blood
And here, the land is in the bones.

The night-strong scent of elderflower
The nightshade and the monkshood cowl
The embers of a cooking fire
The starlight in my mother's blue-black hair
Where Honeysuckle wove a bower
And knowing well how late the hour
The nightjar and the silent owl
The piping bat, the prowling cat,
Passed by to see them there.

For heroes need their homes again;
So many lost; those who remain,
They too have wives to love,
And travellers do not complain,
They shrug away the evening rain
And make the heath their hearth as on they move.

While far away, yet not too far to hear a nation cry
And drawing ever closer by the day
A shattered winter city where the tramlines score the sky
Amid the girder'd chaos knitting broken spires and domes
Broken windows, broken roads and broken hearts and homes.
The searchlight dims
The Child draws breath
The Earth draws the curtain on her festival of death.

My mother loved my father in a valley by the sea
And all these years away the world has still so much to learn
They lie beneath the primrose, the forget-me-not, the tree,
And I shall join them.
When it is my turn.

Cornwall 2007

PARKS HIS FERRARI

Parks his Ferrari alongside the takeaway
Stilled by the ocean that ripples and curls...
Marriage is anodyne. How might he break away?
Killed by emotion he gazes at girls.

Sun-tanning leisure as far as the eye can see,
Fragrant the zephyr and topless the beach
'Is there no pleasure,' he sighs, 'for a guy like me?'
Vagrant, it ever remains out of reach.

Downing a beer: feels the alcohol soften
Dread of the morrow. The thread of the pain.
Drowning his sorrow, a thing he does often,
Empties the bottle and orders again.

Beer mats are crushed. A mellow hour passes...
Nothing is rushed at this time of the year.
Heel-taps stain yellow a number of glasses.
Time for a snack, then, and just one more beer.

Chews a kebab with a pickled zuchini...
Swears by the sand and the sun and the sea,
'Give me that Bint in a hint of bikini!'
Slopes to the Gents for a much-needed pee.

Flexing his pecs he critiques his reflection.
Not unlike Elvis, the form in the glass...
Loaded with sex in the denim's perfection,
Thrusting his pelvis, he tightens his arse.

Left espadrille makes a tentative foray;
Out through the doorway with unsteady grace.
Brute in pursuit of a little Amore,
Smile of the hunter creeps over his face.

Setting his course by his dangling medallion
Careless of deckchairs and toddlers and towels
Women alert to this angling stallion
Mindful as mice in a cageful of owls.

Oiling her thighs lies the targetted vision
White is her waxing and golden her tan.
Seemingly casual with deadly precision
He sits, this relaxing inebriate man.

Charming, disarming, in chatting-up fashion:
'Hullo my Darling, I've met you elsewhere...'
Smarming, alarming, 'You fill me with passion...'
Answer: 'I don't! And you haven't, so there!'

Taunting attack! Feeling soberer, sillier...
Ego is pricked like a plum with a knife
Haunting the voice; there is something familiar.
Takes off her Ray Bans.
My God, it's his wife!

Grabbing the towel he covers her nudity,
Chides with the words of a son of the soil;
Cool as ice-cream she reproves him for crudity,
Slides off the cover and hands him the oil.

Gleeful the holidaymaking fraternity
Schadenfreude rampant. Discomfited male!
Nine months elapse to a happy maternity
Mended the marriage and,
Ended
The
Tale

Saint Ives, 1960s

37

SO THIS IS DEATH.

So This is Death.
The avalanche of cards has stopped.
The organ din, the candle blaze
The laudatory golden haze,
The kindly comments on one's days and, legacy...
The Tea. Pink, dreadful ham to eat.
The cost of pleasure and deceit:
The frost
When black-suspendered wives and girlfriends meet...
Cruel tableau of Erotic Gothic fantasy.

So This is Death!
The oddly slowed-down dread has stopped,
The screeching, tearing forward thrust,
The splintering, the blinding dust
The sudden crush that, surely
                        Must have broken me.
And yet, the pain is fully real
And I can see, and, (Help me!) Feel,
The screaming bones upon the buckled steering wheel
For reeling, pulsing life has not forsaken me.

So, This is death.
Your awful rasping breath has stopped.
Such silver hair. Your final sweat
Still beaded on the brow that yet
Will soon be cold as butcher's meat.
                      My memory:
Of riding on your shoulders,
(I, the child
Above the Easter hedgerows, high
As heaven in the racing, bracing smiling sky)
Returns to taunt anew Aghast Reality.

So <u>This</u> is Death.
That brave and loving heart has stopped.
Your intellect, that left me cowed;
The lovely voice that cried aloud...
Is muffled by your winding shroud.
My darling girl, I'd rather not have viewed you so,
The Undertaker's mockery
Of everything that love should be!
I was so wrong to think that I could bear to see
Or try to kiss the twisted lips that once kissed me.

So This is Death?
And everything at last has stopped:
The Ego's weight was very strong;
The nagging, hurtful inner song,
That told me I was always wrong.
I fought it, but I have to say, it wearied me.
And in ten years; or, less than three
The people that I loved (or, heedless, harmed) will be
The only ones that, good or ill, remember me.

So. This is Death:
With every breath, lest it be stopped
We must give thanks that we're alive,
And where we can, help others thrive,
And grateful, LIVE, not just survive.
The gift of life surpasses all totality
And every second that I waste
In selfish gloom, unkindness, thoughtless haste...
Adds darkness to the house of my mortality.

So: THIS is Death.

London 2008

THE LONG LONGING

When I was small;
When I was new and empty
Easily seduced
By sweets and windmills,
Treats and toys;
The melancholy
Sun-green woods
Of hard High Summer
Called to my longing.
Rustled my longing
In their mortal leaves,
Cried to my unknown longing
In their late, last
Birdsong-pierced
Bat-fluttered
Lingering twilight;
Shadowed my bowels
With watchful, wakeful
Hateful, wet-eyed,
Yearning, ignorant
Pyjama-sweated moons
And school-shy, burning
Dandelion-idle,
Cricket-shirking noons.

And since my Longing
Gained an adult heart
To wrench and quietly sunder,
This it does with practised ease
Under the thundrous, Wondrous Summer air.

I rub awareness raw
Across the jagged edge
Of broken-hoped despair
To prove my own existence
And all my sea-cloud high,
Sun-washed, shell sounding,
Sea-cave-hollow summers
Haunt like mirrors down the Rhythm of the Will Divine
Persisting and rehearsing
My yearning-echoed Longing
For the first and final Summer
When, yielding to life's tide,
I know My Home
Is really
You.
The early lunchtime sun
Makes diamonds
Of the dust upon my window.
The sun-green leaves
Are cracked and dry,
The singing shell confounded:
Surf-pounded shapeless shards
The shades of Art.
Blessed though I am,
I cannot find,
(Cursed as I am, nor bring to mind)
My way across the sky
Nor reach or, hope to reach
My home within your heart.

Riviére du Loup 1979 Quebec

WHEN EVERYTHING IS
OVER SAVE THE WEEPING

When everything is over save the weeping
When time, the healer, seems too slow to heal,
When grief's exposed the lie 'Not dead but Sleeping'
When sorrow is the only thing that's real,

Then softly comes the love that must transcend
The love of lovers,
The greater love supernal, there since time was first begun:
The love that deep within our very inmost heart discovers
The light that shines eternally and, guides us to the One.

The music lies un-played; though understood,
The Lyric left unsung:
Silent is the theatre, hushed the stage.
For you and I shall fade; not just the Good,but
The Fortunate die young;
Spared the awful miseries of age;

We perish.
But, the deeper love that makes of life
A work of art
Shall cherish here that loveliness: Forever in my heart.

Aston Cantelo 21st Century

EPIC VERSE

EPIC VERSE

THE HISTORY OF OUR NATION
AGES
THE GREAT ANON
"I'M HUNGRY!" CRIED ADAM

To qualify as Epic, a poem must be a longish narrative on a serious subject, rich in events that are significant to a tribe or culture, spiced with heroic deeds.

Well, my subjects are serious - indeed Ages and "I'm Hungry" are grimly apopemptic and merit the safety-valve of a little laughter.

Heroic?

Well, few lives are devoid of heroism, even if such events consist less of the bloodied sword, more of confrontation in the dark silences of the soul with those agonies of conscious change that make us who or what we are. But yes, there is blood.

What is for me a long poem wouldn't fill a footnote to Homer's Odyssey, but these three each exceed in length the other verses in my work, and all three embrace the 'Once upon a Time' factor that defines a Story.

I understand that Epic Verse should correctly be composed in Dactylic Hexameter. For those as ignorant as I was, Tennyson's "Half a league, half a league, half a league onward" comprises three Dactyls and a Spondee and is most certainly Heroic.

Scholars may debate whether this metre with its onrushing hoof-beat intentionally mimicked the gallop of a legendary hero's horse in the ages before Tennyson.

I will be content if these verses are read to reflect the speech-rhythms of our time.

Cornwall 2014

I've stolen, from the "Lyrics" chapter, a song I wrote in the Nineteen Seventies for Thames Television's "History of the Ballad". This was an engaging piece of didacticism rolled in entertainment in which I played a Neanderthal, a Viking, a Troubadour, a Tudor court composer, a seafaring Balladeer, a London Busker, a Post-Punk Popstar and a Space-Voyager; "THE GREAT ANON" was the Title track, and although it's nowhere near long enough for epic status, it DOES deal with the on-going deeds of its eponymous imaginary hero over a protracted period; from the dawn of our culture to the future, both as perceived through the lens of that culture nearly forty years ago. The origins of a huge amount of our heritage are anonymous, and often the more intriguing for that reason.

THE HISTORY OF THE NATION

Is NOT peaceful integration,
But an accurate account of brutal force.
How it overwhelms the Meek,
As the Roman screwed the Greek,
And Everyone got rogered by the Norse.

Picture; you're indigenous, you farm your fen... Uliginous,
Odiferous and sodden though it be,
You are distant from the lairs
Of those scary wolves and bears
In the Forest. SO much safer by the sea...
But Look, my Child! A whale? No, a pretty, stripy sail!
Then another... And the dragon-headed ships
Of the Hornéd-Helmet Hordes
With their axes and their swords
Howl in. And little chap, you've had your chips.

You're a mark, for you're a man. The invader has his plan
And it won't encompass sparing you your life.
You'll be Pierced in the subclavian
By some randy Scandinavian
Who'll celebrate by pleasuring your wife.
The fundamental dicta are that spoils go to the victor,
And the maid may NOT resist the Regis Rex.
The bloodline of your village?
It's the fruit of rape and pillage
For the Bad Boy is the one that gets the sex.
Success IS procreation; Ghengis Khan begat a nation,
And whether you're the cream or you're the dregs,
It's less about your charm or, the muscle in your arm
And entirely what you've got between your legs.
On the plumper plains of France,
Rather smarter Danes advance;
They've worked out one doesn't kill the golden goose;
As long as they get paid, (and as long as they get laid...)
They'll go away and leave you on the loose.
In Paris, Charles the Bald was annually galled
For Geld, by yearly fleets of armed marauders.
He chose the cleanest bunch and, inviting them to lunch,
Proposed a little deal to hold his borders.
'Come. Settle 'ere by me!' He said; 'I'll give you Normandy,
A pleasant spot, as you may go and check.
If you become a Norman, you can function as my lawman;
Just keep Les Autres Bâtards off my neck!'
Within a generation, they were Frencher than the nation
That they'd colonised instead of laying waste.
They turned their dread Protection into legal tax-collection,
The racket that STILL leaves a funny taste.
No need to get a fix on the year ten sixty-six:
Duke William enforced his Droit Majeur...
Harold scanned the sky and got the arrow in his eye.
It's stitched: on the Tapissery Bayeux.

Now: of any two, the Crueller will naturally be Ruler,
The line is fine 'twixt terror and respect,
And between respect and awe it's still finer,
And what's more,
Is embraced on both sides more than you'd suspect.
For healthy domination is a part of education,
Building character, depending how one copes...
Getting sodomised at school is a VERY useful tool;
By one's wedding-night one sort of knows the ropes...
And thus were forged the chains
Of a thousand years of reigns,
With the Peasants dispossessed and in the mud
And the Monarchs in their palaces
Begetting, with their phalluses
The Heirs to carry on their Royal blood.
Remarkable to tell, it's worked out rather well,
A Status more than Quo the State enjoys.
Who wants dull elections while the King still gets erections;
And the Queen has healthy babies that are boys?
While elsewhere the inbreeding
Led to chins that were receding
And the miserable bleeding of the heirs,
Here the ritual beddings (and occasional beheadings)
Led to weddings that just led to more affairs.
Abroad the institution fell to bloody revolution
In lands where monarchs formed a narrow breed,
Here they're tolerated, for it seems we're all related,
Having all participated in their seed.

We're sprigs, or something ruder,
Of some Stuart, George or Tudor
Or a by-blow of some other Royal Faux-pas
(That there's been so little sin, Sir,
In the ruling house of Windsor,
Is a triumph of the Palace's P.R...)

For Royalty holds sway right until the present day,
And we're spared the Presidential staff of hacks.
Though it's surely common sense
To consider the expense,
They only cost us tuppence on the tax.
Are they out of touch? Well, does it matter much?
While Figureheads no longer plough the storm,
The tourists get excited
And we all love getting knighted...
More affection than Protection seems the norm.
You may feel like throwing rocks
If your home's a cardboard box,
But when monarchs are deposed you see too late
The egocentric faces of Dictators in their places,
Whose wicked sons will spoil your Nation State.
The Tabloid-reading Panickists
Are terrified the Anarchists
Are going to kick our Royals up the arse.
Me? I've only one complaint,
And it isn't that they're quaint,
It's the fact they're all so bloody Middle-Class.

Longleat, 2011

AGES

ONE

Perception: Fuddle, Muddle. Sleep and Wake and, Feed;
(And Nipple, Suck, and Cuddle, are all I want, or need.)
Comfort, Love and Mummy, Toes and Fingers too,
And, Rattle, Bottle, Dummy, and Nappy, Pee, and Poo...
Cuddle, Coddle, Fiddle; Potty, Presents, Pram,
Then Waddle, Toddle, Piddle ... Perception: Shit! I Am!!

TWO

I am a conscientious Child. My infant crimes are few,
My socks are clean and strict routine enforces all I do.
It's ABC and Jam for tea, and Punishment and Pain:
Pronounce your Vowels, control your Bowels,
(And wash your ears again)

THREE

In Formative Grey Flannel, a scholarly defeat
(Examination Panel versus Cricket Team Conceit)
The freezing knees of winter and
The itching summer heat.
My balls have gone all hairy, and I've size eleven feet.
And now I'm smitten with procrastination
I scarcely have a grip on any situation
I vacillate, equivocate, my shoulders scarcely grown,
Mistaken for my Mother on the bloody telephone.

FOUR

I try to strive for virtue, but how? When it's such fun
To do the thing I shouldn't
With the should-thing left undone-
I ought to spend time studying;
And, must I watch my weight?
Oh, Bread and Bed, I worship thee! Athletics, thou I hate!
And now I hear an awesome cry across the pointless years:
"Drop out! Rebel! Consign to Hell the values of your peers!"
I lie mute in my bedroom. I can hardly see for tears.

FIVE

Boots. Dusty on the cracked, white road.
Sun. Hot upon my skin.
Gone; my money. Lost; my watch.
New; whiskers on my chin...
The Denim tight about my crotch: the Tiger loose within.
Thrill me. Shake me to my soul! The hot adrenaline
Runs tingling down my fine young veins.
A fig for Discipline!
The distance beckons, Blue above.
Come, play the Harlequin,
And, young forever, there goes love.
How soft, how sweet, is Sin.

SIX

But....
Suddenly I'm Not So Young, and now I see the light!
And everything I once did wrong, guess what? I get it
right.
I rise with robins nicely, precisely like the sun;
From six to eight: I meditate, from eight to ten: I run.
From ten 'til two I earn my due, and then I take a shower
And then I do aerobics for three quarters of an hour
And then I do my paperwork from three till half past four
While sitting in a Lotus on a Futon on the floor
And when each book is balanced
and each cheque is neatly crossed
I telephone my friends
and tell them how much weight I've lost.
My mind is transcendental and my body like a clock
And I speak to every lentil
As I boil it in my Wok.
I Cycle, and I'm Celibate; I use organic soaps

But.......
Time brings greater wisdom and maturity, one hopes..
For: when you gain enlightenment, the purest form of Zen
You can come down off your mountain
And embrace the world of men
Where, Abstinence, we all know, is the Novice's conceit.
One doesn't draw attention to the sandals on one's feet -
It's better far to own a car, and eat a little meat.

SEVEN
I'm....Middle-Aged; and movement can be something of a
chore
And all that Self-Improvement. Does it matter anymore?
I wake up when it's handy, and no-one gives a hoot
If I breakfast on a Brandy and a Singapore Cheroot.
My tailor forms my figure, for I give my guts no quarter
As I lunch
with some sweet creature young enough to be my
daughter.

I'm overdrawn. My banker can shout and tear his hair
but we all know he's a wanker, and I can't pretend I care

It's fine to drive a Bentley, if there isn't too much traffic;
It's fun to watch a video. Who says it's pornographic?
It's grand to snooze til tea-time, and then, before I dine,
From six to eight I fornicate, and if I can, til nine,
When, seated in the carver with the linen at my throat
We'll rampage through the a la carte and, trash the table
d'hote
Then we'll drink until we're merry and we'll smoke until we
snore
And I know I'm not an angel
But at least,
I'm not a
Bore.

EIGHT

Upon my soul, I'm growing Old!
I Feel it, in my skin; Through cracked blue lips
Too slack to keep the spittle from my chin.
Where once I'd wield the rapier, it's more a, safety-pin...
I dine tonight by candlelight
On sardines from the tin.

NINE

Perception: Fuddle, Muddle. Can this, really, be?
Where did I put my spectacles! Without them I can't see...
Do I have to take my pills, or do I have to pee?
Where did the Golden Autumn go, my fine declining years.
(I lie mute in my bedroom. I can hardly see for tears)
Am I then, Not enlightened.
Is that why I'm so Frightened?
I haven't used you well, dear God, but...
Is there Hope for me?
I always thought there'd be more time before the final spin
I die tonight
By Candle-Light.....

Please,
Will you take me in?

Highgate 1989

THE GREAT ANON.

Have you wondered who found the Words,
Who set them into Rhyme...
Who was that somebody, un-deterred
That stole the melody from the bird?
Borne on a whispering wind half-heard
Soft through the mists of time.
Who made the songs that come down to us?
When fortune, wealth and fame
Have turned to dust – as all things must –
With a long forgotten name...

WELL:

I'M THE GREAT 'ANON' (BOOM BOOM)
I'll tell you: Once upon a time,
That every Balled, Verse or Rhyme, each Ode or Elegy,
Every Jingle, Song or Sonnet
        With no Author's name upon it
Can be blamed upon 'Anon',
ANONYMOUS that's me!

        I'm the raconteur, Troubadour and Jongleur,
        For Rhyming, Mime and, Timing
        Were an aid to Memory
        Until my Verse was writ in Runes
         And Tablature secured my tunes
        To suit the Lute, the Flute, the Spoons!
         (RACKETY-TACKETYTACKETY-TACK)
        ANONYMOUS that's me.

I'm the Balladeer and I come from Far and Near,
I've travelled down the centuries and sailed the stormy
sea...
I've hunted Buffalo, fished for Whale,
     I've been in Love, (I've been in Jail!)
AND ON, ANON, STILL RUNS MY TALE,
ANONYMOUS that's me...

     I'm the raconteur, Troubadour and Jongleur,
     For Rhyming, Mime and, Timing,
     Were an aid to Memory
     I've marched with soldiers, on the day
       That heroes turned to mortal clay,
     I've rolled the maidens in the hay!
     (ANONYMOUS that's me.)

I'm the great 'Anon',
But my time is nearly gone,
For printing and recording redefine posterity
I've been arranged in all the keys,
     Collected in Anthologies,
And No-body said so much as 'Please'....
ANONYMOUS.
        That's me...

London 1978

'I'M HUNGRY!' CRIED ADAM

"And the LORD God said, He must not be allowed to reach out his hand and take also from the tree of life and eat, and live forever."

'I'm Hungry!' Cried Adam,
As belly and bone felt the stirrings of first appetite.
'I'm Hungry!' He cried,
'I am: hollow inside...'
Adam counted his teeth with his tongue.
The feeling was new and the words were untried
For the barely-made man was so young
And, aching for something to bite.
'I'm hungry!! I'm hungry!!! I'm hungry!!!! I'm Hungry!!!!!
I'M HUNGRY!' He wailed to the Night.

God smiled like a child,
No longer alone on the ledge between darkness and light...
'I'm happy!' He mused and,
Beheld the half-grown of the image (his own!) with much joy.
A girl freshly smitten receiving a kitten
Could not have thought more of the boy,
Though fully aware of his plight.
'Might do him again with a little more brain... But,
He's Hungry! How splendidly Right.'

'Behold!' Said The Logos
'These things to delight and sustain you
And muscle your girth...'
'I'm hungry!' Sulked Adam;
But then he caught sight of the lettuce, the pendulous berries,
The leaf and the shoot and, the succulent root,
The Tubers, the Goobers! The Cherries...
The foodstuffs of infinite worth;
His virgin seclusion engorged with profusion,
The beautiful fruits of the Earth.

'I wonder.' Said Adam
Replete and, excreting his first ever stools in their plainness
And kicking asunder
The ordure stuck under his foot on the sweet orchard floor
Returning the spoil to the generous soil,
Concerned to be clean as before,
(And, thinking his excrement heinous)
Lacking a teacher, he scooped up a creature
And, used it for wiping his anus.

The creature ran, fuming
Obsessed with its grooming, affrighting a nose-licking cow.
'I may be a Bunny,
But that wasn't funny!' He squealed at his tittering mate.
And taking the cue – as they usually do –
The sheep edged away to the gate
Where, taking his ease 'neath the bough,
Even the bear in his plentiful hair
Considered Man warily now.

'I'm lonely...' Said Adam.
'Please send me a friend that's not stupid,
Not hairy, not mute?
Fragrant, and beautiful,
Helpful and dutiful, something to cuddle at night;
Something not Brute, but a little Astute?
(Nyah... some of the sheep were alright...)
I think I've made up a word: "Cute."
We've sorted the Faeces, now let's try the Species?'
(...Here, Comus looked up from his lute.)

And, God was indulgent;
'I think I might have what you need...' He regarded the youth,
Entered into his mind
Determined to find something nearer perfection and bliss.
Toyed with some features the creatures enjoyed,
Awakened the thought with a kiss
And, visualised beauty, forsooth!
Ordered the Plenitude, sculpted the Void...
And, made them a lot less uncouth...

'I'm weary,' cried Adam
'Of waiting around...' and he slept as a babe, free from care
On the ground and quite nude,
Not feeling the rude breath of night
And immune to the cold.
'When you're older,' Thought God, 'well...you may not elude
The effects. You do not, when you're old.'
And Adam slept on, unaware.
The blue Lunar light shone, bright with delight
Awaiting the fruit of his prayer.

And God's mighty fingers
Ran over the feet and the belly, the head and, the glans.
Then, moving discreetly
Felt into the thorax and swiftly located a bone;
Severed it neatly, and healed it completely
Adroitly withdrew the genome...
Worked for an age on the plans.
(And you in the Tomb, how dare you presume
To assume that God's time is like Man's?)

The Dawn blazed in splendour
And Adam's limbs stirred in the dew as he slowly came round
And, dazzled lay blinking
As God's Gift gazed: thinking and,
Flicking her hair in the sun.
'I feel really odd...' She glanced up at God,
'May I ask, what this IS that you've done?
God smiled and uttered no sound.
'You mean' she said dryly, 'that THIS is the one?
This rough, naked boy on the ground?'

'I'm Adam.' Said Adam,
Attempting to rise, and, bewildered and somewhat in fright
He widened his eyes
And,
Forming the new words for Bosom and Bottom and Lips
Cautiously hiding the bruise in his side,
Stared amazed at her legs and her hips.
Stirred and bewitched at the sight;
Said, he also felt odd - He peered up at God,
'My Winkle's stiff! Is it all right?'

'I'll try not to smile'
Thought Eve; 'I'll allow he has VERY nice buns
And good pecs.
But what to do now?
How vacant his brow!' Here, she gave him a tentative prod
With her toe, to repeat the effects.
Said Eve, 'he's so Stupid, dear God!'
I've seen that his penis erects
But where, when you want him, is Cupid, dear God?
This boy hasn't EVER had sex!

In the following weeks
She laboured profoundly,
Constructing then cleaning their nest
While the man sat around,
Enjoying the sound of her singing.
As months became years,
Her energy spent, she became discontented,
Her songs often choked by her tears.
And here I'll indulge a cheap jest;
She whimpered her fears, but they fell on deaf ears.
'Twas the Sabbath, and He was at rest.

And now we leap Forward;
For everyone knows of the Winesap, the Serpent, the Scene...
A story for children...
Yet one that bewilders. Just what does the metaphor find?
That God made mistakes with the sex and, the snakes?
That man should decline his own mind?
That some of God's work was unclean?
May I remind the unkindly-inclined
That the World is both Seen and: Unseen.

'I'm hungry!' Cried Adam.
And God shook his head.
'I'm afraid,' he replied 'no more treats.
You know Good and Evil.
I'm sorry,' He said. 'But you did what I said you should not.
You screwed up, I fear. The instructions were clear.
It's a pity.
I liked you.
A lot.
Your utterly wretched deceit
Has done for you now. By the sweat of your brow
You must labour in order to eat.'
And next, here's a strange thing:
God curses the land! A supremely irrational act
And, hugely un-Godly.
But somewhat more oddly, observes,
(and to Whom or, to What ?)
That 'The man has become like Us.' Not "One" but, "Some"...
As they say, this sure thickens the plot.
From what might such knowledge distract?
Why keep it hid from the Idiot Kid?
It suggests that the Deity's cracked.

A crazy Creator
That's able to dream the sublime and miraculous Earth?
Design and begin it,
And everything in it; and then next the minute: a curse?
Tantrum and Pet aren't what one hopes to get
From a mind that's Divine. It's perverse
And hardly the stuff of re-birth,
A chapter and verse one would flinch to rehearse...
And it doesn't do much for self-worth.

For God must be flawless.
But Angels, on record, are certainly known to have flaws.
Not all can be trusted:
They fell and, they lusted, which sadly discredits their race -
Any demon you like could be grabbing the mike
To speak in the Deity's place,
For devils adore making laws...
So: hearkens your Prophet to Heaven or Tophet?
It should, as they say, give one pause...

For, which would you rather?
On this hand, the Father, on that: the Mad Uncle of Hate...
So thus down the ages
Through pages and pages, monstrosity stalks like Alastor.
Prepare to draw breath; have a Life. Get a Death
It sure makes it tough for the Pastor.
It pitches one's faith against fate;
First the oblation, then dread depredation;
Atrocity lying in wait.

I need to write faster
Or else to leave out a significant chunk of the poem.
It is time to condense
Yet how to make sense of the story of all since the dawning?
Adam's descendants, his seed and dependants;
You see in the mirror each morning
The sperm of one offspring alone:
Such grief for a mother! Her son killed his brother,
The Other that never came home.

'I'm angry!' cried Adam
And belly and bone felt the welling of feelings unknown
In the garden of joy
Where an innocent boy knew only the love of his mate,
For men hearing voices will sometimes make choices
That lead them on pathways of hate
Where Evil grows wings like a Throne;
Where mother and daughter will speed to the slaughter
The sons of the foe and, their own.
Soon many were dying.
With fast multiplying comes vast competition for food
And always man finds
A way to win minds,
When there's plunder and rape in the bud
And uses God's names for his personal games
And deems it not wrong to shed blood
Indeed, he claims God thinks it good.
Hence, the Sinning, the Flood, the Pharaohs, the Blood,
The Blood and the Blood and the Blood...

'I'm Needy!' Cried Adam
As man got a taste - with inelegant haste - for excess
And, greedy for gain
Made it perfectly plain
That he wanted far more
Than his share.
What suave Being spoke to an average bloke?
(You should check whom you trust with your prayer)
And said 'Happily, We acquiesce...
My Dear One, of course. You must take it by force!'
...And we come up to date, more or less...

Where, little by little
Man yields Aaron's Rod to a knowing and powerful clique
And little by little
Man murders his God. At first as act of defiance,
Taking a poke with a thin, nervous joke;
And finally, slays him with Science,
Endorsing the mean, winning streak.
The bitter perfection of Natural Selection
Leaves nothing at all for the meek.

'I'm Hungry!' Cried Adam,
And belly and bone lost the home for the mortgage arrears
While the huge MNCs
Starved the birds and the bees
When the last of the trees were cut down
None stood in the way of the chemical spray
For the few final fields were long brown,
And hadn't borne fodder for years.
'I'm Hungry!' Cried Adam across the Macadam
And far off, God's eyes filled with tears.

Cornwall 2014

THE DAMNATION FILES

THE DAMNATION FILES

THE HORRIBLE TRANSMOGRIFICATION OF LITTLE
MISS MUFFET
THE ARCHITECT
THE BARRISTER
THE COLUMNIST
THE BISHOP
THE IMPORTANCE OF FAME

My earliest influences did not have massive gravitas.

Later, I had the pleasure of hearing Brian Patten, Dannie Abse, Adrian Henri, Adrian Mitchell and Jeni Couzyn who often read at 'Pentameters', a terrific little poetry salon upstairs in the unheated Hampstead of the 'Sixties, where I was the resident guitarist. My late first wife Charlotte and I lived in Tom Stoppard's old flat in Vincent Square. I had the pleasure of knowing Charles Causley and Laurie Lee; dear Roger McGough the Patron Saint of Poetry came to the launch of 'Farmer Fisher' at the London Zoo. One might have hoped for a little of all this quality to rub off, but Wordsworth was right. The child is father of the man, and Edward Lear, Lewis Carroll and the obsessively perfect Hilaire Belloc were already ingrained too deeply.

Add in the Music-Hall rumpety-tump that permeated the stages under which as an infant I so often slept, and you will see that I was vaccinated against the Sensible in the Arts until life taught me via surprise jousts with grief and sorrow that comedy is licensed to address the most grievous of subjects.

Several writers have produced cautionary tales for the childish errors of the present day – mine will appear under separate cover – but (except for the egregious Miss Muffet whose surreal come-uppance belongs here) the Damnation Files tackle the sins of Adult Professionals.

For now I will leave out my profiles of the Politician and the Banker (and may well omit the Artist) as these subjects have now gone way beyond the reach of satire.

Severe Divine Retribution may be the only solution.

Cornwall 2014

THE HORRIBLE TRANSMOGRIFICATION OF LITTLE MISS MUFFET.

Little Miss Muffet said,
'Bub, you can stuff it! I won't eat it. Take it away.'
Distressing the waiter presenting the plate
of the Chef's Special Curds of the Day.
Persisting with calm to conceal his alarm,
He protested the charm of the sweet.
She straightened her arm, obtruded her palm
And spilled it all over his feet.
'Let me make myself plain,' said this Gluteal Pain,
'If you wish to remain in your niche,
You'll fulfil my design, or your job's on the line.
Now get me a burger! Capiche?'
The waiter - whose pride was displayed in his stride -
Squelched away in a murderous mood.
Determined, let's say, to gain face for his tray,
Sent away in a cab for such food.
Now between you and me, the man had a degree
And was nicely informed on nutrition.
He waited, you see, as a struck off MD,
- Some complaint of coercive coition.
          The burger was brought - of a popular sort,
It reposed in its polythene box,
Where steroids compete with debatable meat
To repeat the physique of the ox.
Miss Muffet fell to with a gusto quite gruesome,
A twosome could not have dined faster;
It's bad for the soul to swallow things whole.
For the body it's total disaster.
Deprived of relief, the hormonal beef
Sent a chemical jolt through the nerve-vine;
'Build muscle!' It said. 'On her hips! On her head.
And don't rest till she's perfectly bovine.'
Customers swooned as the moppet ballooned,

A-wobble with blubbery shudders;
It wasn't her size that was such a surprise:
It was rather the horns and,

>The Udders.

But what of the staff?
Well, they just had to laugh;
As Miss Muffet made helpless cow eyes,
She had quite overlooked the spider, half cooked
That arrived:

>In the box.
>>With the fries.

My Child, be polite.
You know it's not right to be overbearing and rude.
And if there's there a moral...
It's best not to quarrel with people who handle your food.

Lausanne, 20th C

THE BARRISTER

Larry was a lawyer, though he wasn't very good.
He left it to his Junior as often as he could
To do each day what found its way into the tray marked
"IN",
And when there was too much, well;
Why not drop it in the bin?
It didn't really matter if the verdict went astray,
For Larry was a partner and; they paid him anyway.

His hours were not demanding, and his duties often small,
And he thought of his profession, if he ever thought at all,
As a splendid occupation for a man of modest skill,
For even when he cocked it up, he still sent in his bill.
It didn't really matter if the client saw the boss,
For Larry was a partner, and he didn't give a toss.
He gained his wig and gown - in fact he even had his silk:
The school his father sent him to, with others of his ilk
Was just the place for networking and, other sorts of play
That took place in the dormitory; an ambience parfait.
It didn't really matter if one batted or one bowled;
None ratted on a partner, and one's partners never told.

Promoted as a prefect he enjoyed a sense of power -
Indulged his little defect with the matron in the shower,
Connected with his studies and corrected with the cane
As beauteous bosom buddies, for there's pleasure
Where there's pain...
It didn't really matter or divert him from the joys
Of leaping like a satyr with the other Naughty Boys.

And so to University; and though he had to part
With his Partner in Perversity, it didn't break his heart...
And when his final papers were not his year's worst,
The board of covert capers awarded him a first.
It didn't really matter, but it aided his career
He started as a partner, and the road ahead was clear.

He gained a predilection for a certain sort of friend.
They mostly met in special clubs in parts of the West End.
The world of Crime and Punishment was lovingly discussed,
And they charged him by the hour, as professionals all must.
It didn't really matter or affect his livelihood,
For Larry was a partner, and his partners Understood.

Now, when you're next in Mayfair, you must picture,
If you can,
The undistinguished ending of a mediocre man.
Emerging Bastinadoed from a basement, it was thus
That Larry tripped and left this life,
Run over by a bus.
It didn't really matter what his next of kin endured,
For Larry was a partner, and; handsomely insured.

His soul, of course, was naked, and became a mite confused
As he thought of Madam Whiplash,
Where he'd lately been amused;
And as his mind grew darker, so he started to descend
Until he heard a voice say 'Ah; so *there* you are, My Friend...
It doesn't really matter; shall I flatter with a term?
I know that you're a partner; but of course: not in THIS firm.'

Larry's spirit rallied: 'Well, to Hell with the expense!
I'd like to phone my Junior to fax down my defence.'
The telephone was quickly brought, but no response ensued,
And Larry hit the brimstone, still embarrassingly nude.
It didn't really matter that his Junior didn't phone,
For she'd been made a partner, and her time was now:

Her Own.

Highgate, 20th Century

THE ARCHITECT

Archie was an Architect. He had a happy life,
Devoted were his daughters and attractive was his wife.
He had the right connections,
Whose affections helped him thrive.
A most exclusive motor-car sat smugly in the drive.

His shirts were made to measure by a man in Jermyn Street
Another made the calfskin brogues
That gleamed upon his feet
He lunched at Bertorelli's, and the Ritz provided tea,
Which left an hour or two for work conveniently free.

His haircut was immaculate, his fragrance subtly male
And he kept a lissom mistress at a flat in Maida Vale.
He liked to drink and gamble, just as frequently as not,
And had a place upon the Hamble, handy for his yacht;

But home, of course, was Hampstead, and,
His house was Home indeed,
Designed by the Victorians, fulfilling every need.
Fine windows let in air enough,
And filled the rooms with light,
And Archie found it fair enough to sleep at home at night.

It's sad when starving foreigners from mortal life retire,
It's horrid when the homeless hypothermically expire,
And everybody's sorry when a dog has had his day,
But how much more upsetting
When the prosperous pass away!

One bright autumn morning on the lovely Finchley road,
Archie, yawning, failed to see a lorry shed its load.
A wrench upon the steering wheel, a screech of tyres on tar
And Archie was a write-off.   Too bad about the car...

Archie's soul leaped upward with an angel and a thrill,
- His daughters trashed the furniture;
They couldn't find his will -
'Welcome to Eternity,' his escort said with grace,
'For such an Architect as you, we've found a special place!'

And now came many faces; and a noisy, lightless power
Compelled him grimly downward to a grimy concrete tower,
Through an awkward portal with a smell of sick and dirt
And down a dismal passage with a colour scheme that hurt.

The freezing wind whipped in and out
And flung the garbage high
And dreary and identical, and blocking out the sky
And hulking to infinity and bulking all around
More gloomy towers of concrete loomed
Upon the lifeless ground.

The lift was claustrophobic and a horrid place to be in
As all the drunks who used it thought it suitable to pee in.
Out along the stairwell with its dizzy nightmare drop
Archie's escorts dragged him till they reached the very top.

They showed him to a little room upon the hundredth floor
With cracks in all the windows and graffiti on the door
And, though so high,
The urban sky was black with fume and smoke;
He cried, 'Yes, well, I've seen enough.
You've had your little joke!'

They said: 'these towers are thought of well;
We didn't think you'd mind them...'
He shouted 'What? This place is hell! And, who the hell
designed them?'

The demons (for that's what they were)
Made Archie's door secure.
'Why, YOU did, Mr. Architect;
As housing
For the poor.'

Highgate 20th Century

THE COLUMNIST

Jimmy was a journalist,
He lived a life of bliss.
(He wasn't a reviewer, or I'd not be writing this!)
Waiters leaped at his request
He tipped them like a lord
And always ate the very best his paper could afford.

Jimmy and his cameraman were often to be found
In beautiful resorts with lovely people all around;
Notorious or famous, it was all the same to James
Reptilian and squamous was the calling of the names
And, meted out in platitude. His Attitude was sound:
Banality designed to strike the punters as profound.
He cried, 'The truth can't hurt you
And from truth I'll never flinch!'
And sold his outraged virtue at a mighty column inch...

For James was not a nincompoop,
His head controlled his heart
A fellow in his income group would naturally be smart
No simple Court Reporter could afford to live as he:
He specialised in slaughter and, was paid accordingly.
He blamed his unnamed sources
And created through his tricks
Some milkable divorces and, a suicide or six
A chiller in a villa or a Bentley in the ditch
Our writer was a killer and he preyed upon the rich.

And when he'd drained a scandal to the final bitter cup
He'd happily mishandle facts
Though NEVER make them up...
Within his chosen area of cleavers knives and fleams
Just like a pit bull terrier
He quite enjoyed the screams,
But as for tapping telephones He NEVER listened in
On private conversations that concealed a public sin
And as for active bugging, why, he wouldn't even ask!
Abundant were the paid informers gagging for the task.

His moral anaesthesia made his friendship somewhat risky,
So when he had a seizure with his seventh double whisky
The boozers in El Vino's
Shrugged their shoulders in their macs
The losers in casinos felt entitled to relax...
And there we leave the Beautiful. It wouldn't be remiss
To follow Jimmy dutifully down the dark abyss...

He went, for his improvement, to a chamber lined with eyes
At every little movement
They expressed their shocked surprise
While disembodied voices with the kindness of a blade
Passed comment on the choices of redemption that he made.

And as for recreation, while the demons and their friends
Kept minute observation thru' a telephoto lens
They'd make him run and later, read the mail and the sun
But never "The Spectator", for compassion there was none.
And every seven years or so
They'd mock him him where he sat
And let him earn his tears as a laboratory rat where,
Locked inside a maze he'd lose his reason and his hope
Until they sliced him open underneath a microscope.

And thus throughout eternity he squirms beneath the eyes
He treats with taciturnity the liars and the spies
He's even due remission if he's able to survive
A position as a hedgehog on the old M25

But, in the name of pity
(And it hurts to hear him plead)
Can no one in the city send him something good to read?

Highgate 20th Century

THE BISHOP

Brian Was a Bishop, and a worthy man indeed.
He had a passing fondness for the candles and the Creed,
Though hazy on the Scriptures.
Who, today, has time to read?
For the ways of the world are strange...

He liked to dress informally, preferring to be seen
In a simple cashmere sweater and Designer denim jean.
In fact he feared the gaiters looked a shade...
Well; epicine,
For the ways of the world are strange...

His easy social manner pleased the Canons and the Dean
And even charmed the Organist, a Maid of sober mien;
She learned to strum the banjo
While he thwacked his tambourine,
For the ways of the world are strange...

He blurred Commandment Seven for his liberal Diocese.
Communicants supped seated. It was kinder to the knees
And stressed that Genuflexion's
For the French and, Portuguese...
Well, the ways of the world are strange...

He spoke of Self Denial, but with tact and subtle stealth
While stressing that pure Spirit often goes with fiscal health...
Somalis don't repair you roof.
You need your men of wealth
In this world where the ways are strange...

He died and, went to Hell at last, as many have before,
Like every English Bishop since the days of Thomas More.
Not one has gone to Heaven.
Not since Fifteen Thirty Four,

For the ways of the world are strange...

Brian wasn't bothered. 'Fact he took it very well:
The sights and sounds unnerved the man, but happily to tell,
He'd been a secret smoker.
So, he didn't mind the smell.
(Well, the ways of the world ARE strange...)

He joined a mighty queue with poets, anarchists and kings.
The demons took his finger-prints, his mitre and his rings
And danced around him wearing them
And singing 'Favourite Things'
For the ways of the world are strange...

But when he reached the turnstile they said rudely
'On yer bike!'
'We're chock a block with Bankers,
Politicians and the like.'
'If we let you in as well the little sods'll call a strike!'
For the ways of this world are strange...

Brian looked for Limbo, but in fact it wasn't there,
So with horrible anxiety he climbed the gilded stair
And went up to Saint Peter with his fingers in the air
(For the ways of the world are strange...)

To Brian's vast amazement Peter smiled, 'Hullo old chum!'
'Go in and make yourself at home,'
He jerked his saintly thumb...
'We're mighty quiet at present,
He'll be awfully glad you've come,
From the world where the ways are strange!

A blinding light. A mighty voice:
'MY BOY, HOW VERY GOOD
IT IS AT LAST TO MEET YOU!'
Brian quivered where he stood
And faltered,
'But I don't believe in You. I never could,
In the world where the ways are strange!'

The Mighty Voice was merry,
'WELL, WE'VE PUT THAT RIGHT AT LEAST'
'BUT I THINK YOU'LL BE UNCOMFORTABLE
AMONG OUR POOR DECEASED.'
'GO BACK AND LEARN YOUR LESSON
AS A SIMPLE PARISH PRIEST
IN YOUR WORLD WHERE THE WAYS ARE STRANGE.'

Brian thanked him kindly and departed in a state
And plunged back down the staircase
He'd so wildly climbed of late.
The demons shrugged their shoulders
As he hammered on their gate...
Oh, the ways of the world are strange and strange,
Yes, the ways of the world are: strange.

Highgate, 20th Century

THE IMPORTANCE OF BEING FAMOUS

Littlejohn Artistic-Worth
Was blessed with talent from his birth
When he was two, the little mite
Could effortlessly read and write
As well as most grown-ups can speak
In English and in ancient Greek:
And nor was this his only skill,
From studying with Roland Hilder,
He'd a grasp of brush technique
That left Paul Rubens looking weak.
As for his dry-point engraving,
He'd have had the critics raving,
If it weren't for father's whim,
ÖBut later on we'íll get to him.

Littlejohn, though barely four,
Conducted Brahms without a score,
With Simon Rattle not much worse.
And nor was he behind at verse;
He wrote a terse and seminal poem
On the work of Theobald Boehm
And thus inspired by wind and wood
Could naturally be understood
To have a truly pressing need
To play upon the beating reed.
The Oboe and Bassoon indeed.
He also learned the Ophiclede.
His repertoire for this alone, ten compositions of his own
In all the usual Tonic keys –
Plus some employed by the Chinese
Quite outshone his fine transcriptions
Of the songs of the Egyptians
All this in so young a child should have sent the critics wild;

So now I'm sure you'll want the crap
About his fathers handicap:
It's simple really; to his shame
He had a low regard for fame
And feared that if his son were tainted
Nothing that he played Or, painted
Could be judged upon its merits.
Like a mouse pursued by ferrets,
Littlejohn would never know
The peace to let his ideas grow;
So the lad was kept sequestered
Making sure he'd not be pestered
While he wrote his timeless prose
Composing these
And painting those.
The tutors cost a grand a day;
How he wished they'd go away!

See the spaces on the wall,
The threadbare rugs, the empty hall,
How else to keep the Bank at bay?
Papa looked strained, Mama turned grey,
But both agreed it was a joy
To educate their brilliant boy.

Littlejohn, when, then, he grew to manhood
Took the useful view
That publication of his stuff
Would probably bring in enough
To keep his parents from the street.

He thought the idea pretty neat
Till agent after agent cried,
(And slapped his thigh and clutched his side;)
'WHAT did you say you want to do?
Why, no-one's ever heard of you!'
Showed him the door and sent to press
The negligible ghosted mess
Of Debby Pleb, Celebrity.
Though just a child to you and me,
A fool unschooled, she nonetheless
Made quite an educated guess
At just how much the papers pay
The sort of bimbo who'd betray
a member of the Cabinet.
She's living on the proceeds yet,
A botox multi-millionaire,
Whose implant boobs, false nails and hair
And tattooed bottom – do we care?
Are on the chat-shows everywhere.
And Ian Posh? he's famous too,
And un-resigned; (they never do)
The scandal helped him keep his seat
Where cottaging had risked defeat.
While driving drunk, he smashed the car
Of Nobby Blockhead, soccer star
Accorded fame for throwing up:
Believe it! In the F.A. cup!
Cocaine in Spain, too much champagne,
And whoops! celebrity again!
The moral is, and you can bet it
Unless you're famous, just forget it.

Littlejohn cast up his eyes
To Heaven. 'Try a painting prize!'
Said Reason. 'It's well known the Turner
Is a Doddle. And an Earner.'
Littlejohn took up his paints,
And dashed off some Renaissance saints,
A dreaming landscape, and a nude
Like Ruskin in erotic mood.
Ouvres to match the Louvre in Paris;
Better, even, than Rolf Harris.

Gutted, sad and sorely vexed,
That year, the next year and the next,
Naturally he didn't win.
But this time, looking pinched and thin,
He made the shortlist; it was said
His masterwork would knock them dead.
What a concept! Simply vast.
And Cutting Edge! He had, at last
Purchased, for an un-named price,
A thermo-nuclear device,
Strapped it on and kept his date
With the Committee and, with fate.

His fellow artists stood like this,
Their offerings of shit and piss
Applauded, but; they had to learn,
This year was not their Turner turn.

The whole committee rose as one,
As flashlights froze their favourite son;
Each one struck a rapturous pose and,
Frozenly embraced the chosen.
Littlejohn, among the faeces,
Blew himself and, them, to pieces.

In the deepest pit of hell,
Littlejohn is doing well
Honour shines as honour must;
Parole has even been discussed.
He won, of course; but in his heart
He wonders,
           Was it really:
                         Art?

Highgate, 20th Century

POLEMICS

POLEMICS

FOR ENGLAND
PIGGY-BACK
ORGANIC PANIC
TWELFTH NIGHT
HOLLOW HALLOWEEN

Are these verses Polemics? The Greek *polemikos* means "warlike, belligerent..."

and polemics are usually written to challenge – indeed, annihilate - existing positions and opinions with little concern for the feelings of those that are challenged.

As I have grown older – an achievement for one that in his youth had little concept of safety for himself or others – I've found it harder to dip my pen in the acid that fuelled the battery-cells of my satirical career. I have become woefully kind at many levels and tho' I still enjoy Target Shooting can no longer deliberately harm living creatures, either with lead or, ink. Nevertheless, these verses are designed to unsettle.

If they do, then I have succeeded.

Cornwall 2014

FOR ENGLAND
(MORE HOME THOUGHTS FROM ABROAD)

ENOUGH
Of chili spice, of rice, delights of coconut and ice,
Of latitudes where urgent plans
Are languid, like the ceiling fans.
Here, in the hazy afternoon, so lazy in the warm lagoon
I'm years away from fog and frost
And falling slates and, rising cost,
From aching joints and gloomy days
From frozen points and long delays.
And yet...and yet, I can't forget: My glum old homeland calls.
The worn and dirty Dover cliffs and,
Rolling-roofed Saint Paul's
Half hidden - and with little heed –
By shameless monuments to greed
In debt for things we'll never need
Until the curtain falls.

OVER
The bridge of time, my mind
Leaves the spoilt city's grime behind:
A dog-rose at the slanted edge of sunlight in a tangled hedge
Transports me to a country road,
Where once I played at Mr. Toad
In some lean, booming English car, Lagonda, Allard, Jaguar
With walnut-bordered, dancing dials
To clock the leaping English miles...
And yet, and yet, did I forget? The years of strife and pain,
The signpost at the crossroads, the lifeblood down the drain
The Spitfire shriek across the tar, the empty places at the bar,
The friend who'll never need his car,
The flowers in the rain

THEY
Never saw the death of worth, the burning trees,
The threatened Earth;
Was it for this our wasted seed gave blood and limbs
And, lives?
                              I read
Their names on faded, poppy'd stones
Of glorious village heartbreak.
                              Bones
That played upon an English field
Increase some distant dunghill's yield.
The high ideals for which they rest
Have - clearly - still to manifest:
And yet, and yet, lest we forget, effect and cause we serve:
The drugs, the dirt, the thugs, the hurt,
The shocks to heart and nerve;
On freedom were our children fed and,
Not sent supper-less to bed.
Forgive, this day, such daily bread...
                    We get what we deserve.

Singapore 1984

PIGGY BACK

I wish I was young and attractive
I wish I had come-to-bed eyes
Then I could be sexually active
With People I really despise.
In London or Paris or Venice,
Show me the scandals I'll sire!
Famous for four-poster tennis;
So! Envy, respect and, admire -
A Duchess, an Actress, a Diva,
I'd keep them enchanté for days
And streak through St. Marks shouting
Viva! ...Delicto Flagrante, It pays.
And when you get hurt by my capers
Follow my method, please do:
Just dish all the dirt to the papers.
:) That's why I'm richer than you.
But, when I've played B*ggar my Neighbour
With sycophants, rather than friends,
And bonking's my day-to-day labour,
What The F**k would I do at weekends?
Ticketed in Wikipedia!
Babes, aren't you wondering how?
Show Your Bare Arse to the media,
I'M A CELEBRITY NOW.

Mayfair, 2001

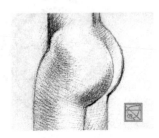

94

ORGANIC PANIC

Organic crops, to quote some wit,
   Are grown by Hippies, using
      Sh...
         ovels,
           Forks and other hand-held tools
To shift the decomposing stools
Of
 Horses, Cattle, any beast; it doesn't matter in the least.
Indeed, but for the EEC,
They'd use the Doos
      Of you and me.

The produce of this pagan mess
Looks dull, mis-shapen; nonetheless,
When scrubbed and scraped with tempered edge
Tastes marvelously fruit and veg,
A tribute to the loving land.

Big business, on the other hand,
With chemicals and clean machines,
Grows Perfect Plums and Gorgeous Greens
And,
Like some archetype of Plato's:
     Perfect spherical potatoes,
       Fresh as any Starbucks muffin,
       Firm and plump and taste of:
             Nuffin

Cornwall 2005

TWELFTH NIGHT

Sitting by the fireside I placed another log.
Merry sparks burst cherry red.
The flames renewed their power,
Gleaming on reflected richness, rare antiquity
Treasures that affirm my status and prosperity.
In my glass a mellow malt. The coldness of the hour
Prowled outside. Nearby I heard the barking of a dog.

Ding dong went the door chime;
Guests weren't due yet at my door...
Testily I called the staff; did no-one hear my call?
Thundrously a knocking came
That shook the Christmas tree.
Angrily I called again, 'Is no-one here but me?'
Sullenly I left my chair and shuffled down the hall.
On the step a stranger stood. Dishevelled, young and poor.

Irritably I enquired his purpose. By what right
Did he dare disturb my easy comfort and my peace?
Silently he raised his eyes and looked me up and down,
Taking in my slippers, my cigar, my dressing-gown...
Nastily I mumbled about calling the police.
Sadly he regarded me and moved into the light

Eyes of fire held mine and I was helpless in his gaze...
Tales of ancient mariners came flooding to my mind
Samuel Taylor Coleridge? But this man was not malign.
Quietly he shook his head. Again his eyes met mine,
Reaching out he took my arm, a gesture not unkind.
He and I were travellers. We walked alone for days.

Here the sea and there the sky. They blaze, two setting suns...
Softly, winter wraps a silent night around the hill.
Felted clouds release their snowflakes on the naked trees.
Huddled hard upon the frozen higher ground one sees
Shadowed figures, moving in unease or lying still...
Whimpering, a child in terror dreams a dream of guns.

Where the village?
Where the park, the school, the hearth, the home?
Only bones beneath the snow remember where they stood,
Buildings that affirmed a faith in higher things above,
Beds where once grew flowers,
Beds where bridal pairs made love,
Cushions, books, utensils, toys, is nothing left that's good?
All are crushed, to lie with broken hope beneath the loam.

Tenderly my guide now spoke. His voice was warm and low,
'If you'd be remembered, Friend, and, if you'd save your soul,
Know: a man's not measured by his net financial worth.
Use your wealth to help the helpless, everywhere on Earth
Think on this and, think on me; for soon your bell will toll.'
Standing shaken on my step I never saw him go.

How long did I shiver there? Intrusively the cars
Drive up. They break my waking dream. My guests are many.
Put away the tinsel and the reindeer and the elves.
Are you troubled for the poor, or only for yourselves?
And I? How many years to make amends are left, if any?

Awkwardly they wonder why I weep beneath the stars.

Cornwall 2011

HOLLOW HALLOWEEN

"LOOK! What lovely pumpkin lanterns grinning by the door!
Eyes, and teeth! So real! – but
What's that dripping on the floor?"
Hush my child, and come away
They're the fruit, I'm sad to say,
Of bonuses for Bankers,
(And Parliamentary wankers)
Whose billions came from taxes
ON THE LABOURS OF THE POOR.

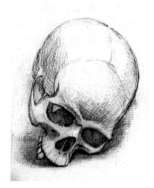

LYRICS

LYRICS

A TRIVIAL AFFAIR
APRIL IN JULY,
EARLY FOR THE TIME OF YEAR,
NOT TO BE,
ON Y VA,
RIDE AWAY,
THE BOUNCER,
THE YOU I THOUGHT WAS YOU,
YOU ARE MY HOME,

The LYRE was and, still is a very simple stringed instrument capable of producing Chords, and thus like our not-infrequently abused Guitar, good for the easy accompanying of sung verse. The ikon of the lyre used as a cap-badge by military bandsmen is pretty, and suggests that the original was made by tying a cross-bar near the tips of the recurving (and excised) horns of something like an Ibex and stuffing the root ends into the leg-holes of a large tortoise-shell. Strings were fixed to a peg in the creature's tail-hole, stretched up across a bone bridge on its flat belly-plate and, wound around the bar. According to an authority I consulted when illustrating a book on very, very early music, the strings were 'twisted with raw skin and fat' in order to tune them*.

The tortoise-shell was intended to resonate as the Lyre's sound box. Remove most of the Tortoise first, and its shell will do as required producing a mild amplification that sounds, to my ear, both hollow and thin. But, Classical Greeks were not accustomed to the warm sonority of later western European instruments, and compared to their Aulos, a primitive oboe that required the player to wear cheek-bandages in order to force enough air through the screaming reed, the Lyre must have sounded heavenly. Apparently it was always played with a plectrum "WHICH WAS TIED TO THE INSTRUMENT WITH A LENGTH OF RIBBON OR SIMILAR, TO SECURE AGAINST LOSS". I put this quote in capitals for those contemporary musicians that may benefit from the information.

Lyric poems, I am told, usually express the feelings of the writer and are "traditionally in the present tense." Some of mine obey these rules.

The first lyrics I wrote were infantile comedy fitted to melodies popular in our roving household. They therefore possessed a Cowboy twang and, the metre suggested hoofbeats.

I soon discovered a gift for melody, and it feels a little traitorous to expose any of my lyrics here stripped of their tunes, for all are set and many recorded. But, this is not a song-book.

Cornwall 2014

It was this appetizing image that inspired the bluebottle drone accompaniment to my short poem 'Flies' which you will find in the section labelled "Pastorale".

Some of these verses are printed with markups for stresses and breathing for the benefit of singers.

All the lyrics printed here are contemporary and their publication in this volume previews their ongoing recording set to the melodies of their author and composer (Ed.) *

A TRIVIAL AFFAIR

It was just a trivial affair...
Simply, just: a trivial affair,
So why this rush,
When someone who is not like you,
Yet really quite a lot like you, goes by...
Who could think a foolish crush
Worth memories that bring a blush,
not I!
Yet, tonight, I had to stop and stare...
It's not right. My heart cries out
"Unfair!"
That love I hoped was dead
Should go and raise its head
When each has made a bed elsewhere...
It was just a trivial affair.

I know when I took your hook;
You gave me that old-fashioned look,
A look that made its meaning crystal clear.

You never said you loved me then,
and there were women, there were men;
And I won't say I love you now, My Dear.

Yet, tonight, I tremble on despair...
It's not right.
My heart cries out
"Unfair!
That love I thought was dead
Should go and raise its head
When you have said you'll wed
elsewhere...
Was it such
A trivial affair?

APRIL IN JULY

It's such a wet July...
The streets are overflowing
Beneath the drenching sky
Our dreams were undefined...
The rain got in my eye...
And suddenly you're going
It's April in July...
The month that is unkind.

I have to wonder why...
The auspices were glowing
Each there to satisfy
A love that seemed designed
So lucky you and I,
And yet the hurt was growing
Not April but, July...
The month that is unkind.

We were surely living in paradise?
What a rare meeting of minds!
But, usual rules apply...
I hear the whistle blowing
It's April in July...
The month that is unkind.

It's April in July...
The streams were overflowing
Beneath a drenching sky
Our dreams were undefined...
Please say it's not goodbye?
There's so much love still owing
To April in July...
The month that is unkind...

EARLY FOR THE TIME OF YEAR

Wild birds are calling, First leaves are falling,
Early for the time of year...
Nights growing longer, Wind getting stronger,
Moisture in the atmosphere...
And I give you thanks, for the boundless days of Summer
When my work didn't have to interfere...
Swallows are flying, Roses are dying,
Early for the time of year...

Once in a while when you're fearful of the night...
Sometimes I catch myself reaching for the light;

Stuff on the wireless, Ugly and tireless,
Nothing that you'd want to hear...
Singers are trying, Statesmen are lying,
Cynical and, SO sincere.
And I know that Now I should start to write my chapter -
Or zip up and, slip out and have a beer...
Judged by the binding, Things are unwinding,
Early for the time of year...

Once in a while when you're fearful of the night...
I have to stop myself reaching for the light;

Broadband's a mess, so: I'll make an Espresso,
Telephone the engineer
Why am I trying? No-one's replying;
You must think I'm never here...
And I wish I could describe for you the mountains...
But I'm waiting for the fog to clear...
Can you hear thunder? Listen and wonder;
Early for the time of year...

...And I see that my in-box has a message
And the smiley-face has shed a little tear, Then there's a kiss,
And you ask, do I miss you?

I miss you very much, My Dear.

NOT TO BE

Douse the spotlight, kill the footlights,
Time to drop the curtain,
Fold away the faded costumes, now I know for certain
There's no more time for me,
Thus fades Celebrity
Lock up, hand back the key, and leave...

What to be or not to be,
And that is still the question...
There once was such a lot to be,
I'd welcome a suggestion

For, still the road is long,
The heart is beating strongly,
Why is it wrong to love
A life of make-believe?

Search the mind for what's behind the sea of empty places,
Pity too the faithful few;
I see it in their faces...
I'd like to carry on,
But once the moment's gone
Time to had back the key and leave...

What to be or not to be,
And can I fight the cancer?
Surely there has got to be
A reassuring answer

For memory is long,
And yes, the will is strong...
Why is it wrong to love
A life of make-believe?

SONG: ON Y VA

No need to tell you, you can guess, what a mess,
Just what a mess it was.
The best objectives, nonetheless, I confess... that yes: it was...
Such fine intentions - And yet we see
Whole new declensions - Of misery...
I offered you a flawed design; I must resign.
I know the fault is mine.
Just mark my mailbox 'gone away', no more to say,
No complication...
But if I touch your memory,
Je t'aime encore, petite Cherie
In some dimension strange to me, you will see, On y va....

How did I make / Such a mistake, /My Darling?????
How to destroy / All of the joy so far...
Mais si je touche ta reverie,
Je t'aime encore petite Cherie
In some dimension strange to me, you will see,
On y va....

The story goes that, once begun, Love must run,
Oh yes, until it's done.
That pain and heartache follow bliss , well I for one,
Can vouch for this
Such early magic - So fine, so brief
So soon so tragic - So soon such grief!
The 'planes go by so high above; And soon you'll fly
Too far away my Love.
Yet in my heart you'll still be here, and always near,
For consolation.
Please file this in your memory,
"Je t'aime encore, petite Cherie"
In some dimension strange to me, you will see,
On y va....

One flat bespeaks a minor key, my hours are free,
And no one's kissing me
I miss your edgy energy, the synergy /that we could be
My finger's tracing - Lines in the sky
My mind is racing - Why upon Why ...
Je crois j'entends encore my love, your wounded voice,
Not, very like a dove...
Pour nous il n'y aura pas Duette, seulment regret
Pour tout les rêves...
But If I spark your memory,
Je t'aime encore petite Cherie
In some dimension strange to me, you will see,
On y va...

RIDE AWAY

His spurs were made of silver but his cloak was black as night
The pale horse he rode was Deathly Grey...
You couldn't see his eyes;
They seemed to swallow up the light
But you knew you'd seen the devil Ride Away -
Ride Away, Ride Away,
You knew you'd seen the devil Ride Away.
Ride Away, Ride Away,
You knew you'd seen the devil Ride Away.

(Jackson cursed his Maker till it made your blood run cold—
He sold his soul for money so they say
They found him dead
Surrounded by his diamonds and his gold
And they swore they heard the devil Ride Away -
Ride Away, Ride Away,
You knew you'd seen the devil Ride Away.
Ride Away, Ride Away,
You knew you'd seen the devil Ride Away.

Little Jenny Cosgrove was just seventeen years old
As wayward and as pretty as the day
She always did the opposite whatever she was told
Oh Jenny, tell the devil Ride Away
Ride Away, Ride Away,
Oh Jenny tell the devil Ride Away!
Ride Away, Ride Away,
Oh Jenny tell the devil Ride Away.

The limousine was silver but its windows black as night,
The powder in the phial was Deathly Grey
They gave the phial to Jenny and they promised true delight
Oh Jenny, tell the devil drive away....
Ride Away, Ride Away,
Oh Jenny tell the devil Ride Away!
Ride Away, Ride Away,
Oh Jenny tell the devil Ride Away.

Her lovely eyes were open, when she drew her final breath
Her tempting lips were colder than the clay....
Her pale hands clutched the needle
And the empty phial of death;
She should have told the devil Ride Away -!
Ride Away, Ride Away,
She should have told the devil Ride Away!
Ride Away, Ride Away,
She should have told the devil Ride Away.

The handles were of silver but the coffin black as night
The silent hearse she rode was Ghostly Grey
The lamps all burned like fire as it faded out of sight
And you knew you'd seen the devil drive away
Ride Away, Ride Away,
You knew you'd seen the devil Ride Away.
Ride Away, Ride Away,
You knew you'd seen the devil Ride Away.
Ride Away, Ride Away,
You knew you'd seen the devil Ride Away.
Ride Away, Ride Away,
You knew you'd seen the devil
Ride Away -

THE BOUNCER

I played with the band till I injured my hand, now I work
On the street of lost dreams......

A,1) Sun-kissed
A-list celebrity
Smoking skunk
In the Ladies'... !!
Post-Punk Drunkard
On Table Three
And it looks like he
Won't be going home...

A,2) Whoa there, Miss,
That's the Wrong I.D.?
You know that
We don't serve babies...
No use flashing
Your thong at me!
You're too young and you Should be going home...

B) Incidental violence
Rupturing the silence
Beamer
With a flashing light
Incremental Sirens
Clearing the environs
Guess it must be
Friday Night...
YES IT IS...

A,3) Un-kissed
A-list celebrity
Snorting coke
In the Ladies' !!
Sad bad Joke
Takes a poke at me
And it looks like we
Won't be going home...

C) One more night
On the street of lost dreams
Love and lies
Hysteria and Madness...
One more fight,
In the heat of extremes
All it buys
Are Injury and Sadness
YES IT DOES!

A,4) So-pissed
A-list celebrity
Chucking up
In the Ladies'... Yeugh!
Mop and bucket.
Don't look at me!
I'M THE BOUNCER!
I should be going home...

B,2) I never see the daylight,
Never get my Pay right,
Muscle with an hourly price
Must be knife and gun-wise,
Live to see the sunrise
Going home would be so nice

A,5) De-pressed
A-list celebrity
Overdosed
In the Ladies'...
Paramedics and A&E,
But it looks like he
Won't be going home...
No, it looks like he
Won't be going home...

8Bars in (A1) (A2) (B) (A3) (C) (A,A, B,inst) (A4) (C,inst) (A5) Coda

THE YOU I THOUGHT WAS YOU

The Fool today is not a happy fool, it seems.
I built a lover from the ghosts of broken dreams
If you don't want me,
Why must you haunt me?
The you I thought was you is not for me.

The words of Sages say that, live and, love, we must.
The wisdom of the ages tells us we are dust...
But Death's no answer,
A silver dancer...
The you I thought was you is not for me.

Once in the Shadowlands a wraith of a chance...
Beckoning deep into the shade
Will o' the wisp, you lead a dangerous dance
The Band
Has played...

Your eyes do violence; they tell me so much more.
They bought your silence time to softly close the door...
So cruel the needing
When love lies bleeding
The you I thought was you is not for me.

I swear tomorrow I shall make a brand new start....
But wraiths of sorrow drape the crepe around my heart
If you don't want me,
Why must you haunt me?
The you I thought was you is not for me.

YOU ARE MY HOME

So the short sad day leaks all its dying strength away
And yields the light /
Into Winter's keeping;
Lamps of comfort glow as on I go past banks and bars
And varnished cars.
See the homeless huddle in their rags
Against the mercies of the night /
Weeping into sleeping,
A ragged ballerina in a gown of shadows
Seamed with tarnished stars.

/Since the hour I /met you, Love,
my /heart won't let me be...
/Tried hard to for/get you, but,
        Your /eyes have haunted /me;
/I know I should /let you live your /life
And, set you free,
 But you're my /home ,
                You /are: my /home.

Fire and sleet and snow,
How slowly frozen rivers flow into the gloom,
Heedless of the city
Where the lovers meet, the diners eat
And sit replete as honeycomb.
Deeper sleep than sleep
A shining street to lead the lonely to the tomb
Needless of your pity
Death's a silver dancer, but the answer is:
The Dead cannot go home

/Even though I'm /learning
 how to /live my life a/part,
/Hammer down the /yearning
lest it /makes the teardrops /start...
/Feel the Lovelight /burning
and its /tearing at my /heart,
You are my home,
                    You are: my home.

Need to make a journey,
 need to ride that midnight train,
Need oh how I need, my Love,
to /see you once again
Even if E/ternity's too short
to still the pain
You are my ho-o-me,
 You are my home

ARTWORK:

INDEX

Lightning Source UK Ltd.
Milton Keynes UK
UKOW04f2050300814

237815UK00001B/34/P